Ideas have never been more valuable, creative advice rarely more plentiful – and machines ever more capable of replacing us. But we have the very human ability to get things right after getting them wrong. It always works if we keep trying. This book is about encouraging you along the way. In four words, the advice that may resonate musically in your head is: "Don't worry, be crappy." You will get there in the end.

Go where the idea takes you and don't stop until you get there

ACKNOWLEDGEMENTS

This was developed with the patient help of many people in the BBDO Guerrero office in Manila. Including: Jo Aguilar, Choi Co, Federico Fanti, Meggy de Guzman, Dale Lopez, Vilma Magsino, Isai Martinez, Al Salvador, Val Villaflor and Paolo Villones who helped create the ideas and illustrations you see here. I would also like to thank many family members and friends, as well as current and former colleagues in the BBDO network who supported the idea and to the audiences in Southeast Asia, the Middle East, and Cannes who were kind enough to listen to me, er, talk crap at least 90% of the time.

IF YOU can't FIND THE BOOK YOU WANT to READ
THEN YOU
(TONI MORRISON)
MUST
WRITE IT

DAVID GUERRERO

THE

CRP

IDEAS

BOOK

MILFLORES

We often hold ourselves back when coming up with ideas. We have the absurd expectation that everything we write down must be brilliant. It rarely is, despite the "Eureka!" moment we have all been taught to expect. We won't have good ideas right away. And thinking we should, can lead to premature celebration or angst-ridden gloom. Best to just keep going. Method is a lot more productive than madness. You just have to stick to the plan. It's not easy because there are a thousand things to distract you. But if you follow an idea long enough, things will fall into place, and the work you do will be a lot stronger for it.

THIS
BOOK
WAS PRINTED ON
PURE
ELEPHANT
CRAP

The book started as a presentation. But it was only on a trip to Sri Lanka when a colleague, Keith Wijesuriya, brought me to an elephant orphanage that the idea of a book came to life. The orphanage sold souvenirs to tourists. And their main product? Paper made from what they had in abundance: elephant dung. It's thankfully odorless. (Elephants like chewing up lots of grass.) And with paper like that, you could only improve on a blank page. The axiom: "90% of everything is crap" also came to mind. Who said that?

90%
OF
· everything ·
is
CRAP

Theodore Sturgeon was a science-fiction writer who once wrote an episode of Star Trek where Mr Spock, played by Ukrainian actor Leonard Nimoy, had a rare on-screen romance. But Sturgeon is most remembered for replying to the charge that "90% of science fiction is crap" by saying: "90% of *everything* is crap." In other words it's a statement that can apply to all creative work – and thus not unique to science fiction. It became commonly accepted as true and now the Oxford English Dictionary lists the saying as Sturgeon's Law.

NINE
OUT OF
TEN
BOOKS
are
NONSENSE.
BENJAMIN
DISRAELI

He was not alone in this revelation.
British Prime Minister Benjamin Disraeli
wrote that 'nine-tenths' of books are
nonsense. George Orwell said much the
same thing about book reviews. And
it seems to be a recurring ratio. We talk
about a Hot 100 and a Top Ten. There are
ten nominees for Best Picture and one
winner. And in many competitions about
10% of the entries make the shortlist.

THE
FIRST
DRAFT
OF
EVERYTHING
IS
CRAP

Even Ernest Hemingway thought his first drafts were 'shit.' But he obviously worked out how to keep going because he wrote seven novels, six short-story collections and won the Nobel Prize for Literature.
So if you feel the same way, you're in good company. And getting something — anything — out is better than holding it in. Just ask an elephant.

THE
NEXT
EIGHT
8
MIGHT BE AS WELL.

John Swartzwelder, of *The Simpsons*, says: "Writing is very hard. But rewriting is comparatively easy and fun." So once you have something written, just do the easier job of re-writing until you are happy with it. Keep going. Because applying what we have learned so far, it may take at least nine drafts to get on the right side of Sturgeon's Law.

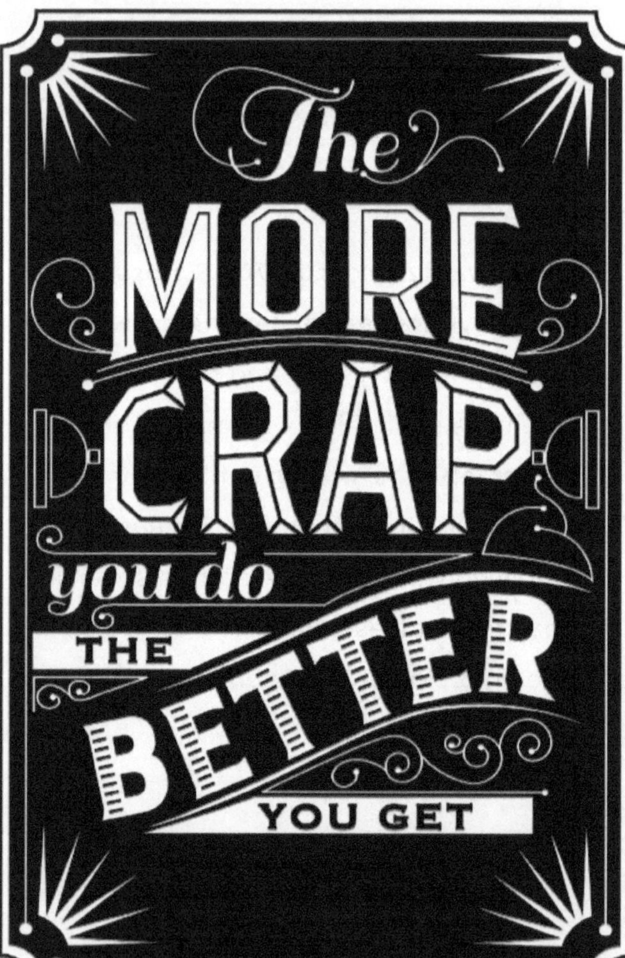

The
MORE
CRAP
you do
THE
BETTER
YOU GET

Scientist Linus Pauling — who followed Marie Curie in twice winning a Nobel Prize— puts it like this: "If you want to have good ideas you must have many ideas. Most of them will be wrong and what you have to learn is which ones to throw away." Most people agree the throwing away is best done later in the process. Have many ideas, go away from them for a while, and then come back and decide what to discard when enough time has passed for you to be objective.

CRAP
IS AN
ESSENTIAL
PART OF
BEING
GOOD.

This freedom to experiment is essential. If you stare at a blank page and refuse to write on it until something perfect pops into your mind, you will be waiting a long time. Better to put everything down — on paper — especially if it's recycled. It's made from all kinds of crap so you probably won't make it any worse. As Barack Obama once said: "If you're not failing, you're missing opportunities." But how do you come up with plenty of ideas? And what should you do with them once you get them?

It's
EASIER
TO TONE DOWN A
WILD IDEA
THAN TO THINK OF A
NEW ONE.

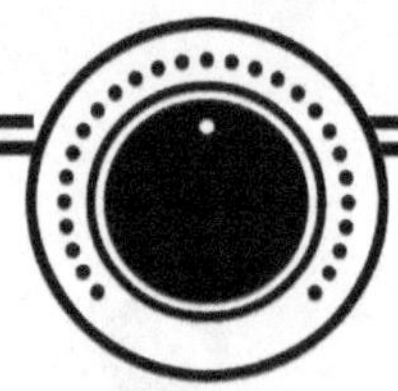

The inventor of brainstorming was a guy called Alex Osborn - the "O" in advertising agency BBDO. He established certain rules of the process to get the most out of it. They include: no initial criticism of ideas, going for a large quantity of ideas, building on each other's ideas and most of all encouraging wild and exaggerated ideas. Write everything down but don't judge them - yet. Come back later and see what works. But just how many ideas do you need?

10%
OF IDEAS
ARE NOT
CRAP IDEAS.
STURGEONS COROLLARY

The optimistic corollary of Sturgeon's Law
is that 10% of everything is not crap. So
instead of worrying about the nine out of
ten things you can't use, be encouraged
by the one that you can. Our job as idea
creators becomes one of coming up with
a minimum of ten ideas - so that we can get
to the one that is not-crap, and then try
doing ten more so you end up with a couple
of things to choose from. And why stop
there?

IF YOU HAVE
100
ideas
THERE'S A CHANCE
10
MIGHT NOT BE CRAP.

When we introduced the line "It's more fun in the Philippines" it became an international phenomenon. People adopted the format and took it in 70,000 different directions. (Including a book: *Advertising. More Fun in the Philippines.*) The line, and what it led to, won the WARC Grand Prix for the "most effective campaign in Asia Pacific." And a decade later it is still in use. And yes, we went through several hundred lines before I came up with the final version far away from the office - while diving in the turquoise blue sea of Boracay Island. An experience I recommend even if you're not working.

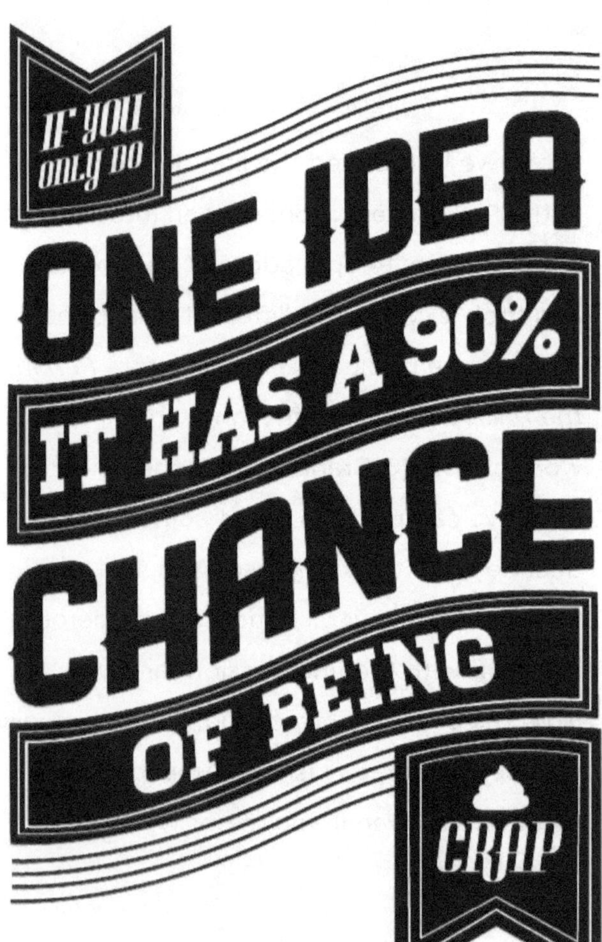

IF YOU ONLY DO
ONE IDEA
IT HAS A 90%
CHANCE
OF BEING
CRAP

There is a critique of advertising that goes:
"first thought." Meaning you started with
something and stopped there. It's probably
not going to be any good. Because it's in
our nature to come up with things that have
already been done, and convince ourselves
we have unlocked the secrets of the
universe. It's possible. But over nine out of
ten times, you haven't. At the start of the
process, it's best to carry on thinking. Later,
it's a race to the finish line.

The Beatles
David Bowie
&
William Burroughs
all used random crap.

William Burroughs, George Harrison, and David Bowie all used the technique of random juxtaposition. We are hard-wired to repeat familiar patterns of thinking. So you need to trick your brain out of them. William Burroughs cut up text with scissors and jumbled the words. David Bowie got a computer to do the same thing. And George Harrison looking for inspiration, randomly opened the *I Ching* and saw the words "gently weeps" which then led to him writing "While my guitar..."

CRAP
SONGS
MAKE IT
EASIER
TO
D·A·N·C·E

It's easier to have ideas when you're not trying to be brilliant. (Amateurs always laugh at themselves. And perhaps the first step of a serious actor is to take themselves seriously.) But when some old disco number comes on, it's acceptable to swing your arms about and claim you are just being ironic. Make the same moves to some cutting-edge remix and you're definitely in Dad-Dancing territory. So pretend you're being stupidly ironic and then you'll find it much easier to get loads of stuff down.

A CRAP JOKE
IS HARDER TO MESS UP THAN A
GOOD ONE.

We don't all laugh at the same jokes.

But we find it easy to agree on a bad one.

Which is why the little one-liners inside

fortune cookies, bubble gum wrappers

and English Christmas crackers are

designed to be as groan-inducing as

possible. You can tell the joke badly and it

only gets better. Next time then, tell

everyone you're writing a really bad idea

and then there's no risk in them laughing

at you — and an even better chance that

you can turn it into something good.

NO
IDEA
IS NO
GOOD

1. Every idea can be improved on.

2. But if you don't have an idea it's hard to improve it.

3. Start anywhere.

4. Do something different.

5. For example:

6. Write your thoughts out as a numbered list.

7. It works for clickbait.

8. It could work for you.

9. Everyone likes lists.

10. You know when they will end.

YOU
CAN MAKE
CRAP IDEAS
GOOD.

We tend to resist formats. Thinking that they restrict our freedom. But weirdly, a structure gives you more freedom to innovate. Peter Souter, a famous creative director turned screenwriter, points out that stories follow certain archetypes—as do Hollywood movies. The convention of three acts, with 40 beats that carry the narrative forward is well established. The same is true of books, songs and commercials. You don't need to tear up formats, you need to refresh them with your own content. This makes stories compelling and easy to relate to. So don't ignore the rules, adopt them and then have fun with the freedom of constraints.

ANG LEE
BELIEVES
his
BEST
WORK
COMES WHEN HE'S
SCARED

I asked Ang Lee what the secret of his creativity was, and he replied that it was "being scared." As a director, his decisions carry the whole weight of a multi-million dollar production. So the maker of *Crouching Tiger, Hidden Dragon*; *Brokeback Mountain* and *Life of Pi* must have been absolutely terrified. If feeling too comfortable is working against you, find ways to leave that zone. Work with the unfamiliar, try what you haven't tried before, and find yourself an un-comfy chair. It might lead to your best work yet.

SCARE
THE
CRAP
OUT OF
YOURSELF.

Just how you do that is up to you.

Deadlines are scary. And we are all,

ultimately, on a deadline. Look at a game

of football. And note how the losing

teams often play best in the dying moments

of the game. Why wait that long?

The first minute is as short as the last.

And it's always later than you think.

IF YOU
THINK
YOU ARE
CRAP
AT SOMETHING
PRETEND
TO BE SOMEONE WHO ISN'T

Galileo Galilei, usually known as Galileo, doubted the entrenched wisdom that the sun orbited the earth. He was the first to prove that the opposite was true.

Naturally, he called self-doubt "the father of all invention." While poet and novelist Sylvia Plath on the other hand, felt doubt to be the "worst enemy to creativity." Neil Gaiman's fix: "if you don't know how to do something, pretend to be someone who does" allows us to gather up some self-belief without blinding us with arrogance.

IT TAKES
10,000
HOURS
of
practice
to
BECOME LESS
CRAP
AT SOMETHING.

Journalist Malcolm Gladwell estimated
the amount of time needed to be good at
something at 10,000 hours. A claim which
has been much debated since, but
somehow took hold in popular culture.
The time involved could be anything from
three to five years. Which is roughly the
amount of time the Beatles spent
practicing their songs before they hit the
big time. So don't expect to do it much
quicker. But be encouraged by the
distance you are putting between yourself
and the next round of competitors.

DONNA TARTT
TAKES OVER
10 YEARS
TO MAKE SURE
HER BOOKS AREN'T
CRAP
(THEY'RE NOT.)

Pulitzer Prize winner Donna Tartt spent a decade on her novel *The Goldfinch*. A typical Pixar movie takes 22,000 person-weeks. (Which might explain why the credits list is so long.) Everything good takes time. The amount you spend on it is an indication of how much you care. And the reward for care is contained in the end-product. Although the line that "A work of art is never completed only abandoned" is one of the most popular in culture - with attributions ranging from Leonardo da Vinci, E.M Forster, Oscar Wilde and to French writer Paul Valéry.

How
LONG
DID YOU
SPEND
ON YOUR
LAST PIECE OF WORK?

There is an often-tested relationship
between money, time, and quality.
Take time and you can stretch the budget.
Rush it and be prepared to pay a premium.
But if a piece of work is both quick and
cheap it will almost certainly be crap. If time
is your most abundant resource, use it. Ditto
with money. The only way to bend these
rules is with ideas people love so much they
will apply a reality distortion field called "get
it done somehow." But use that power
sparingly. Everyone needs to get paid. And
everyone needs to go home at some point.

DON'T GET BURIED in CRAP

Author Jonathan Franzen famously blocked up his laptop's Internet connection with superglue to avoid distraction. These days consider wiping out your Wi-Fi passwords. And turning off all notifications on your phone. You will always have e-mail arriving and people wanting to send you messages. So why not prioritize your time over theirs? You and your ideas could be making the world a better place. And if all else fails, just use a pen and paper. No one can interrupt you there.

A THIRD
of your day
IS ONLINE.
AND YOU KNOW WHAT
90%
OF THAT IS

While reading this you've been added, mentioned or followed — perhaps more than once. And someone has posted something on a group chat you really don't need to read right now. There. We've just saved you checking. Most people with smartphones look at them over 100 times a day. And an interruption as little as three seconds is enough to interrupt the flow of your thoughts. Take a bit of time to take control. Use the settings available to help you focus. Music works to keep you on track as well. Repetitive beats seem to help, as do Bach, Beethoven, Mozart, and, my favorite, Vivaldi.

EMAIL IS
90%
CRAP
SOCIAL
MEDIA
IS, TOO

There is much to be said about how to deal with life online. But recently, writer and actress Michaela Coel put it brilliantly in her Emmy acceptance speech when she said we "feel the need to be constantly visible, for visibility these days seems to somehow equate to success. Do not be afraid to disappear, from it, from us, for a while, and see what comes to you in the silence." Taking control of when and if you appear online looks like a great idea for developing great ideas.

YOU ARE
QUITE
CAPABLE
OF
COMING UP
WITH YOUR
OWN
CRAP

Use your phone as voice recorder to capture your thoughts. Use a word processor to convert speech to text. Use a camera without a phone to take pictures. Use headphones to block out the world. Go somewhere with no Wi-Fi to write down your thoughts. Change your SIM. Disconnect your zoom. Block unknown callers. Lock all known doors. Get stuck in traffic and look out of the window. Go for a swim. A run. A bike ride. Whatever it takes, make time for yourself. It's always time well spent.

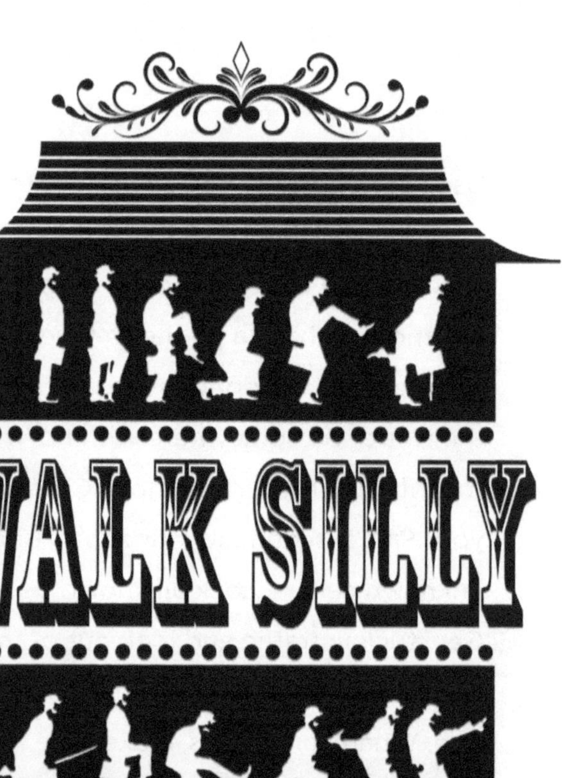
WALK SILLY

Steve Jobs liked to have meetings while walking. And scientists have discovered that walking silly, or in anything but a straight line helps you be more creative. Yes, Monty Python's John Cleese was right all along. A silly walk is better than a sensible one. Exercise silly too. During the pandemic lockdowns, fitness coach Joe Wicks had people lurching around like spiders, crawling like bears and jumping like frogs— probably inspiring great ideas in would-be fitness fanatics around the world.

saying
'NO'
TO EVERYTHING
IS A
CRAP
idea.

In 2012, Eric Schmidt, at the time the Executive Chairman of Google, told the graduating class of UC Berkeley that we should always be opening ourselves up to new things. Among them: foreign travel, fresh experiences, new friends and permissions to access our data. (OK, maybe not that last one.) So try saying 'yes' more often. It can enrich your mind and change long-held perceptions. Of course some think just the opposite: the guy on the next page for example.

SAYING
YES
TO EVERYTHING IS A
CRAP IDEA

Unlike our friend on the previous page, multi-billionaire investor Warren Buffett tells us: "Very successful people say 'no' to almost everything." (Which is probably why he IS a multi-billionaire investor.) Steve Jobs agreed, saying he was "as proud of the things they hadn't done as the things they had." Creative advice is often maddeningly contradictory. You often need to hold opposite ideas in your head and realize they could both be right - at different times. Working out when is half the fun.

BE
CRAP
AT SOME THINGS
BE
BETTER
AT OTHERS

Writer Oliver Burkeman points out we only have 4,000 weeks to play with in life. And you can't be brilliant at everything. So choose what you want to be good at, and accept you will be deliberately average, merely adequate, or outright bad at other things. You may not, for example, be as organized as Marie Kondo, nor as good with dogs as Cesar Milan. But as long as you do one thing that matters to you that's just fine. Focus more and stress less.

Sleep
HELPS YOUR
brain
CLEAR OUT THE
crap.

A team from Boston University has established that while we sleep, our brain gets a deep clean: with spinal fluid clearing out waste that has built up during the day. Neuroscientists have also found that a good night's sleep creates more connections in our brains and improves our memory. So at bedtime, grab some airline eyeshades, turn off the TV and listen to a lullaby. Dreaming beats streaming.

SO
WRITE DOWN
WHAT YOU
THINK
WHEN YOU
WAKE UP
LIKE
RAY BRADBURY

Dreams can be the source of original ideas. Or so it seems. But they tend to evaporate when you wake up. Author Ray Bradbury kept a notebook by his bed. He said nearly all his stories were written from what he remembered from his slumber. And there are others, like author Julia Cameron who believe that writing three pages of whatever is in your head every morning is a great way to build up artistic confidence. There's even a website (search: 750words) that takes that experience online.

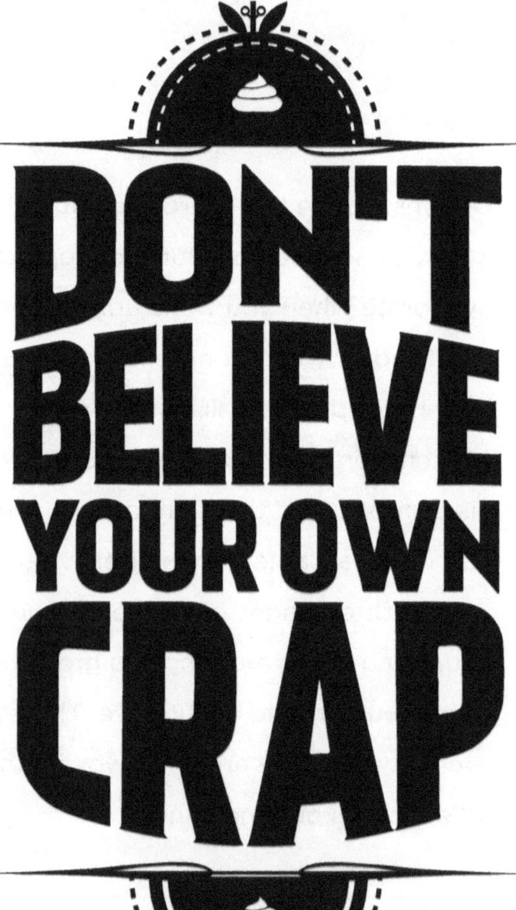
DON'T
BELIEVE
YOUR OWN
CRAP

Nobel-prize winning physicists are as prone to self-delusion as the rest of us. As Richard Feynman put it: "the first principle is that you must not fool yourself. And you are the easiest person to fool." So if you think something is wrong it probably is. And hiding it from yourself won't make it go away. The truth is we have to seek out criticism rather than praise, and test ideas by trying to knock them down rather than prop them up.

·IT'S A·
CRAP
IDEA TO
FORGET
·YOUR·
OBJECTIVE
FRIEDRICH NIETZSCHE

The great German philosopher said that "The most basic form of human stupidity is forgetting what we are trying to accomplish." It's often worryingly easy to do so. How often has your research led you down an hour-long online rabbithole? Remembering our purpose gives us a tool to edit what we look at, and not get lost along the way. Write down the brief, the objectives, and the deadlines. And stick them up where you can see them. When you get lost, they point you back in the right direction.

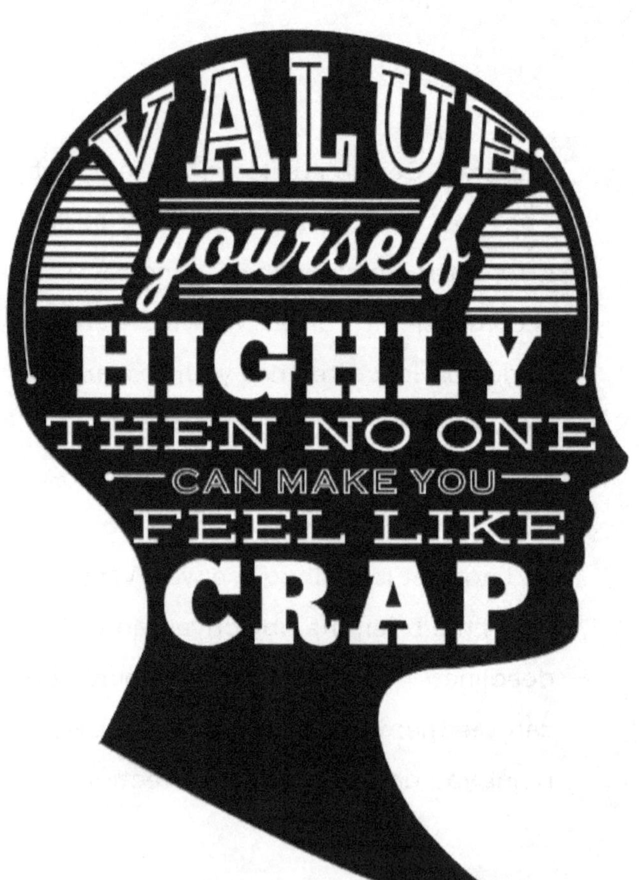

VALUE
yourself
HIGHLY
THEN NO ONE
CAN MAKE YOU
FEEL LIKE
CRAP

As a creative person, one of your first lessons is learning to separate your work from your self. Objectivity will allow you to improve any idea rather than blindly defend it. On top of that, our worth should not be determined by others, but by how much we value ourselves. Partnerships work best on a basis of mutual respect. So if you are still searching for those kind of relationships, keep looking until you find them. Why? Because, as copywriter Ilon Specht once wrote for L'Oreal, you're worth it.

WE ARE HERE
TO MAKE
Life
A LITTLE LESS
CRAP
FOR ONE ANOTHER.

Writer George Eliot had to change her name (and by implication her gender) to get her ideas across. And one of her ideas was the thought that "we are here to make life a little better for one another." How much we are doing so is a good question to ask ourselves - especially if we have access to powerful platforms that can reach millions of people. Be inspired by helping others in whatever way you can: Empathize. Entertain. Educate. Innovate. Improve. We may not always be brilliant. But if we work hard enough we won't be crap either.

Try the
CRAP IDEAS
GENERATOR
AT
CRAPIDEAS.COM

At crapideas.com there are ideas to get more ideas. As well as reviews, updates, notes and comments. Just scan the QR code with your phone. We look forward to seeing you. And thanks for coming this far.

YOU NEED
TO GO
THROUGH A LOT OF
CRAP
TO COME UP WITH A
GOOD
IDEA

ABOUT THE AUTHOR

David Guerrero has spent a lifetime coming up with world-changing ideas. From a tourism campaign that helped double a country's revenue to devising a dissolving, plastic-free shampoo bottle. And making a commercial recognized by UN Women in New York as sparking a debate on gender equality in the workplace. As founder of advertising agency BBDO Guerrero, he has brought home top awards for the Philippines in multiple shows and was the first jury president from Southeast Asia at Cannes Lions. In 2021, he presented a program on the BBC World Service about the time the Beatles didn't meet Imelda. Follow him on twitter @guerrerowrites

DAVID GUERRERO

THE

NO REALLY, YOU DO HAVE TO GO THROUGH A HUGE AMOUNT OF

CRP

TO GET TO ANYTHING LIKE A FINISHED PRODUCT BUT IF YOU KEEP GOING IT IS ALWAYS WORTH IT EVEN IF YOU KNOW YOU COULD STILL IMPROVE IT YOU DO HAVE TO MOVE ON OTHERWISE IT WILL NEVER BE FINISHED

IDEAS

BOOK

MILFLORES
PUBLISHING

www.ingramcontent.com/pod-product-compliance
Lightning Source LLC
Chambersburg PA
CBHW021006180726
47993CB00017B/1109